[FROM A PHOTOGRAPH, TAKEN IN 1858, BY HANFSTÄNGL, MUNICH]

# Franz Liszt

# Thirty Songs

## Edited by Carl Armbruster

### For High Voice

Dover Publications, Inc., New York

## Note to the Dover Edition

In his *Grove's* article on Liszt and his book *The Music of Liszt* (2nd revised edition, Dover, 1966), Humphrey Searle has established dates of composition for some of the songs that differ from those given by Armbruster: "Der Fischerknabe," c. 1845 (this date also holds for "Der Hirt" and "Der Alpenjäger," all three texts being lyrical passages from one play, Schiller's *Wilhelm Tell*); "Kling leise, mein Lied," 1848; "Es muss ein Wunderbares sein," 1857; "Das Veilchen," 1857; "Der König von Thule," 1842; "Der du von dem Himmel bist," 1842; "Mignon's Lied," 1842; "Im Rhein, im schönen Strome," c. 1840; "Oh! quand je dors," 1842; "S'il est un charmant gazon," c. 1844; "Enfant, si j'étais Roi," c. 1844; "Comment, disaient-ils," 1842; "Es rauschen die Winde," c. 1845; "Nimm einen Strahl der Sonne," c. 1855 (the text is by Rellstab); "Die Vätergruft," 1844; "Schwebe, schwebe, blaues Auge," 1845; "Ein Fichtenbaum steht einsam," c. 1855; "Wieder möcht' ich dir begegnen," 1860; "Lasst mich ruhen," c. 1858; "In Liebeslust," c. 1858.

The city of Oedenburg (Ödenburg) near which Liszt was born is now known as Sopron. Pressburg is now Bratislava. The April 23, 1823 concert was actually Liszt's second Viennese appearence. His travels with the Comtesse d'Agoult began in 1835; one of their three children was a son. Liszt settled in Weimar in 1848.

Published in Canada by General Publishing Company, Ltd., 30 Lesmill Road, Don Mills, Toronto, Ontario.
Published in the United Kingdom by Constable and Company, Ltd., 10 Orange Street, London WC 2.

This Dover edition, first published in 1975, is an unabridged republication of the work originally published by the Oliver Ditson Company, Boston, in 1911, in the series "The Musicians Library." A new Note to the Dover Edition has been added to the present edition, which is published by special arrangement with the Theodore Presser Company, Bryn Mawr, Pennsylvania.

*International Standard Book Number: 0-486-23197-6*
*Library of Congress Catalog Card Number: 75-17172*

Manufactured in the United States of America
Dover Publications, Inc.
180 Varick Street
New York, N.Y. 10014

# CONTENTS

# INDEX

# FRANZ LISZT

FRANZ LISZT, probably the greatest pianist the world has ever seen, was born on October 22, 1811, at Raiding, a village near Oedenburg, in Hungary. His father, Adam Liszt, was descended from an ancient, noble family, which in the course of time had become impoverished and had given up its title of nobility. He was an official in the service of Prince Esterhazy, and was himself a highly gifted amateur musician, and a friend of Haydn and Hummel. It was he who gave his son the first lessons in pianoforte playing; and the child was seized with such a perfect passion for this instrument, and his progress was so rapid, that at the age of nine years he was able to make his first public appearance at a concert at Oedenburg, playing a concerto by Ries and an extempore fantasia. The boy's success was so great that his father was induced to arrange a concert, which was given by the young musician himself at Pressburg, where there was a larger public of cultivated art lovers. Here likewise his performance roused the greatest enthusiasm, and several Hungarian noblemen, among them Counts Amadée and Szapary, guaranteed the sum of one thousand florins annually for six years, in order to enable the boy to pursue his studies under a celebrated teacher.

Father and son now moved to Vienna, where young Franz studied the pianoforte with Carl Czerny, harmony with Randhartinger, and composition with Salieri. His command over his chosen instrument grew immensely in the course of a few years; and on April 13, 1823, he played for the first time before a Viennese public. This concert was soon followed by a second one, at which Beethoven was present; and it was one of Liszt's most cherished recollections that the immortal symphonist spoke encouraging words to him after his performance. The pecuniary results of the two concerts were so satisfactory that they yielded sufficient funds for the boy's fur-

ther musical education. Adam Liszt gave up his post, and made the supervision and development of his son's gift his sole occupation; nor was this done from selfish or sordid motives, but purely from his fervent desire to see the boy's efforts crowned with that high measure of success which an adverse fate had denied to his own career. He wished to make of his son not only a great pianist, but also a great composer; and with this object in view he resolved to take Franz to Paris, there to perfect his musical education. On the way to Paris concerts were given at Munich and Stuttgart, which added fresh laurels to those young Franz had already won; indeed, a Munich newspaper of the time greeted him as "the second Mozart."

The father's hopes were fixed upon Cherubini, the stern director of the Paris Conservatoire, and he felt confident that once the latter had heard his son play, he would willingly accept him as a pupil. These hopes, however, were doomed to disappointment, for Cherubini took but little interest in the boy's extraordinary talent, and eventually declared that no foreigner could be admitted to the Conservatoire. Both father and son were for a time almost crushed by this disappointing decision, but matters soon assumed a more encouraging aspect. Two other musicians, Paer and Reicha, who had been present at the interview with Cherubini and were greatly impressed with the boy's gift, did all in their power to atone for the Director's indifference by their most active patronage. Numerous letters of introduction opened to him the drawing-rooms of the best Paris society; the Duke of Orleans (afterwards King Louis Philippe) substantially aided in placing Franz upon a secure footing; and within a short time he was the favorite of the entire musical aristocracy of Paris. Substantial rewards and enthusiastic recognition came to him from all sides, and the papers were filled with his praise. He gave concerts in all the large cities of France and Switzerland, visiting England also several times during 1824 and 1825; and everywhere he was received with acclamation.

Meanwhile Liszt pursued his studies assiduously and indefatigably; and to this period of his life belong his first compositions. During a concert given at Bordeaux his dare-devil temperament once prompted him to introduce under Beethoven's name a sonata of his own; and the deception passed unnoticed. A more important work was an operetta, *Don Sancho*, which was performed at the Académie Royale with great success. Nourrit, the celebrated tenor, sang the principal part, and appeared before the applauding public, at the end of the performance, carrying the young composer in his arms.

It was in August, 1827, that Liszt lost his father, and became, at the age of sixteen, the sole support of his mother, to whom he was devotedly attached. She had accompanied her husband and son to Paris, but had returned to Austria, her native land, after a year's sojourn in the French capital, and taken up her residence at Graz; thence Franz now called her again to Paris. About this time also a love affair, which promised happiness but ended in misery, wrought a great change in the buoyant spirits of the young artist; he turned for consolation to religion, and remained a devout Roman Catholic to the end of his life.

Paganini, the "violin king," as he was called, was then at the height of his fame. He first played at Paris in March, 1831, and Liszt, whose views on art had naturally deepened very considerably by this time, was strongly influenced by the older virtuoso. The great political event of the period, the "July revolution" of 1830, had also not passed without due effect upon him. Furthermore, he had gradually made the acquaintance of most of the eminent French *littérateurs* of the day, such as Lamartine, Victor Hugo, and Georges Sand; indeed, with the latter he was on a footing of great, though unsentimental, intimacy. Yet he did not tire of pursuing constantly the most varied general and philosophical studies; for he became aware that mere talent and its

development is not sufficient for the formation of a real artist's character. As a rule, the great pianists before Liszt had possessed nothing more than a supreme command of the keyboard; he was the first to devote his great technical mastery to a higher object, the expression of the inner significance of music. Having superbly conquered all practical and theoretical difficulties, he realized that the true function of an interpretative artist is to reveal to the public the high and holy realm of beauty.

Naturally, this view found but little sympathy among his contemporaries, who, with very few exceptions, neither understood nor appreciated the sincerity of his endeavors and were still less inclined to share them. Under these circumstances Liszt seriously contemplated, for a time, emigration to America; but the growing intimacy of his relation with the Comtesse d'Agoult (known in wider circles by her *nom de plume* of Daniel Stern) led him to abandon the plan. During their life together she became the mother of his three daughters, Blandine, Claire Christine, and Cosima. Blandine married Emile Ollivier, the French statesman; Claire Christine wedded the author, Guy de Charnacé; and Cosima became first the wife of Hans von Bülow, and after her separation from him, married Richard Wagner.

In 1833 Liszt left Paris, and lived with the Comtesse in strictest retirement at Geneva until 1835; a musical event, the first public appearance and success of the pianist Sigismund Thalberg, then recalled him to Paris. Liszt made his *rentrée* into the arena, and soon won a complete victory over Thalberg; for it was the unequal contest of a great genius with a great talent. A clever critic remarked at the time: "Thalberg is the first pianist, but Liszt is the only one!" The whole world soon endorsed this statement, and it may be said to remain true to the present day, for none of his successors have equalled Liszt's many-sided mastery. In June, 1837, he went to Italy, visiting Milan, Venice, Genoa, Florence, and Rome; in all these cities the same enormous success attended his performances. He remained in Italy until October, 1839, and then began his career as a great travelling virtuoso in right earnest. During the next eight years he visited every European country, and was received everywhere with an enthusiasm quite unequalled. Not only the supremacy of the musician, but also the culture, refinement, and noble character of the man were cordially acknowledged by the whole world. His generosity was unbounded, his unselfish championship of struggling causes unexampled. No needy artist ever applied to him in vain for assistance; sufferers from public calamities, such as conflagrations, inundations, famine, and the like, benefited by his princely donations. Germany owes to him the erection of the monument to one of her greatest sons, the memorial to Beethoven at Bonn, and the citizens of Cologne have reason to remember his generous contributions towards the completion of their famous cathredral.

Eventually, the moment arrived when Liszt grew weary of his life of restless wandering, and when he longed for a permanent home and a more concentrated sphere of activity. In the very zenith of his fame he suddenly surprised the world by abandoning his career as a virtuoso in order to turn to another and a wider field — that of composer, conductor, and teacher. The Grand Duke of Saxe-Weimar offered him the post of Court Kapellmeister, and in November, 1847, Liszt settled at Weimar, where he remained for the next twelve years. His activity in the little town on the Ilm, with its great traditions of Goethe, Schiller, Herder, and Wieland, became of the highest importance, and exerted the most decisive influence upon the whole musical life of the period. From all parts of the civilized world musicians and lovers of music streamed to Weimar, either to become Liszt's pupils, or to witness or assist at the performances conducted by him. As the ever kind friend of rising talent, Liszt produced many new works, which without his help would probably have remained unknown for years to come. We need point only to Wagner's *Lohengrin*, Berlioz' *Benvenuto Cellini*, Raff's *König Alfred*, and Cornelius' *Barber of Bagdad* as the most striking examples. Furthermore,

Liszt revived numerous other works, which were buried in oblivion, among them Wagner's *Flying Dutchman* and *Tannhäuser*; Schubert's *Alfonso and Estrella*; Schumann's *Genoveva* and music to Byron's *Manfred*; Weber's *Euryanthe*; Gluck's *Iphigenia in Aulis, Orpheus, Armide,* and *Alceste*; Spontini's *Fernando Cortez,* and Spohr's *Faust.*

In the concert room Liszt's activity was equally beneficial; for he strove mainly to introduce works which were new to Weimar, and often new to the whole musical world. Nor can it be said that he was at all one-sided in his tendencies, or that his choice was influenced by partiality toward those composers for whose works he had a personal preference; he displayed the most admirable catholicity and eclecticism throughout his career. With the exception of Wagner, Liszt towered above his contemporaries as a conductor, even as he was unrivalled as a pianist.

Taken in its entirety and historically considered, one epoch-making result of Liszt's work at Weimar was that the admirers of Wagner, hitherto locally divided and unknown to one another, first found a definite point of concentration in their endeavors to further the Wagnerian cause; indeed, the great Wagner controversy, which agitated the entire world of music for the next thirty years, may be said to have originated at Weimar. It became the camp of Wagner's friends, and Liszt's personal sympathy with the movement naturally helped it vastly. Wagner has gratefully acknowledged, times out of number, all that he owed to Liszt's friendly efforts.

The most important outcome, however, of Liszt's sojourn at Weimar, was his activity as a composer. Up to 1848 he had confined himself almost exclusively to compositions for the pianoforte. These, being the result of his own technical mastery, are naturally of the highest importance as regards the literature of that special instrument, inasmuch as they are full of original, new, and surprising effects. In Liszt's hands the whole character of the instrument itself was changed. But the forms in which he embodied his musical ideas were as new and surprising as were the purely pianistic impressions. His two concertos and the great Sonata in B minor, although their innate relationship to customary forms is undeniable, yet differ considerably from these. Liszt's antithesis is, as a rule, the outcome of his thesis; or in other words, he works with a principal and a counter-theme, and by their harmonic and rhythmical variation produces his most striking results. In the concertos the point of gravity naturally lies in the pianoforte part, which is of quite unusual brilliancy. His numerous studies form a collection of invaluable treasures for the pianist; they are not mere technical exercises, but possess a deep musical significance, and for many years will be regarded as test-pieces for all those players who aspire to the title "virtuoso." In his ballads, notturnos, valses, and polonaises Liszt keeps to the forms employed by Chopin, though he introduces an individual element in lieu of the national. To the latter he gives due expression in his remarkable *Hungarian Rhapsodies*, which are absolutely unique in character, forming free fantasias on the melodies, songs, dances, and marches of his native land, executed in the most refined taste, with consummate art and exuberant humor. His *Années de Pélerinage*, his *Harmonies Poétiques et Religieuses*, his *Consolations*, and his *Apparitions* are, one and all, charming and highly characteristic. We should also mention his wonderful transcriptions, in which he opens an entire world of song to the pianist; much that the greatest song-composers, Schubert, Mendelssohn, Schumann, and Franz have written for the human voice, Liszt has transferred to the instrument he loved so well. It would far exceed the limits of this introduction, were we to dwell upon his numberless Fantasias on operatic airs, his arrangements of orchestral works (symphonies and overtures), as well as his organ pieces and his critical editions of pianoforte works by Schubert, Weber, and others.

Schumann says: "With talents of the second rank we are satisfied if they command the customary forms; talents of the first rank may even widen these forms; but a genius has the right to use what forms he pleases." When Liszt settled at Weimar the time had come when he claimed this right of genius, and in his later works he undertakes to lead the art of music into new paths by changing the existing art-forms according to his individual feeling. The new works which he created in this sense consist mainly of a number of orchestral pieces, based upon a poetical program to which Liszt gives the title of "Symphonic Poems." Of these, there are twelve: *Ce qu'on entend sur la Montagne* and *Mazeppa*, after poems by Victor Hugo; *Les Préludes*, after Lamartine; *Die Ideale*, after Schiller; *Die Hunnenschlacht*, after Kaulbach's picture; *Tasso, Prometheus, Orpheus, Hamlet, Festklänge, Héroïde funèbre*, and *Hungaria*. The climax of Liszt's activity as composer in new forms is reached in his two symphonies, *Faust* and *Dante*, his two great masses, and his two oratorios, *Elisabeth* and *Christus*.

Concerning the high artistic value of the new art-form invented by Liszt we have the opinion of Wagner, who, after he had become acquainted with some of the symphonic poems, wrote as follows: "I was above all struck by the great, the speaking plainness with which the subject proclaimed itself to me: naturally this was no longer the subject as described by the poet in words, but that quite other aspect of it, unreachable by any manner of description, whose intangible and vaporous quality makes us wonder how it can display itself so uniquely clear, distinct, compact and unmistakable to our feeling. With Liszt the masterly grip in the musical conception speaks out with such a puissance at the very outset of the piece, that after the first sixteen measures I often could not restrain the astonished cry: Enough! I have it all!" Wagner considered this to be so prominent a feature in Liszt's works that he predicted an immediate and wide popularity for them, a prediction which unfortunately is still unfulfilled.

In 1859 Liszt left Weimar and went for a time to Paris, where his mother was still living; then he stayed for an extended period with the Prince of Hohenzollern Hechingen at Loewenberg (Silesia). In 1861 he returned to Weimar temporarily, and then proceeded to Rome. The

Eternal City proved full of fascination for the restless artist, and in April, 1865, Liszt became an Abbé of the Roman Catholic Church, thus to a certain extent retiring from the world. But his admirers and pupils followed him to Rome also; he was ever surrounded by them, and he continued to work for music and musicians in the eclectic and generous manner which was characteristic of his whole life. He remained in Rome for eight years, but from 1869 he regularly visited Weimar for several months in each year. Early in the seventies an Academy of Music was founded at Buda-Pesth, and the Emperor-King offered the post of President to Liszt, who accepted it; there in February, 1876, he entered upon his duties officially. Honored, admired, and loved, as perhaps never an artist before him, Liszt spent the remaining years of his life alternately at Rome, Buda-Pesth, and Weimar. He died at Bayreuth, July 31, 1886.

At this point one branch of Liszt's activity deserves special mention, all the more because it seems to the writer that it has never been sufficiently appreciated by the world in general; it is Liszt's work as an author. His essays on the Goethe Foundation at Weimar, on Wagner's *Lohengrin* and *Tannhäuser*, on Frédéric Chopin, on the music of the Gipsies in Hungary, on Field's *Nocturnes*, and on Robert Franz are excellent in every way, and it would be difficult to name similar works which could bear comparison with them. Quite apart from their brilliance of style, the wealth of ideas displayed, and the author's depth of insight into the subjects treated, these writings confirm the noble quality in Liszt's character which made him ever ready to support with the weight of his influence those men of genius who had remained misunderstood or unappreciated, or to break a lance in defence of their works against apathy, indifference, and ignorance.

. .

Concerning Liszt's songs, it is difficult to determine with accuracy the date when each was composed. Some of them possibly belong to the earlier portion of his career, but by far the greater number are identified with a later period, for it was not until he had settled at Weimar that he gave musical expression to the voices of spring, of love, and of all those sensations which had remained dormant in his mind. This chronological peculiarity must not be overlooked. While Schubert, Schumann, and Franz aspired to gain laurels in the domain of song early in their musical careers, Liszt turns to lyrical composition in the period of full maturity. What he may have carried in his heart for many long years, he produced only after considerable hesitation and deliberation. Doubtless his incessant travels were partly the cause, and only after he had found a permanent home at Weimar could he give himself up to the contemplation of his inner self, with the result that he burst into song. It is but natural, therefore, that his songs differ essentially from those of Schubert, Schumann, or Franz. Upon the pure soil of German song, which so often touches the deepest recesses of the heart, Liszt did not feel altogether at home; his Hungarian descent and French education prevented him from quite becoming a German, however powerful the influence which the works of the great German masters exerted upon him. He ever remained a stranger to their dreamy contemplation and self-concentration. Liszt does not dream, though his fancy is unbounded. His genius produces vivid pictures, full of life and brilliantly colored; but he does not know those sweetly mild dream-figures, those half-mysterious twilight formations, which rise and fall in the poems of the great German poets. His forceful brush delights in depicting only the great contrast of light and darkness, and in this he displays the overwhelming power of truth. Thus his songs are the emanations of his peculiar organization, of his phenomenal technical mastery, and of his Titan-like command of musical expression. If we miss in them the wonderful spontaneity of Schubert, the dreamy pathos of Schumann, or the deep sentiment and formal perfection of Franz, then, on the other hand, they offer us new charms through the declamatory element, which is their special and characteristic feature. It is as if we had entered into a new world, full of well-nigh magic enchantment. In his *Mignon* and other settings of poems by Goethe, in his *Loreley*, *Die drei Zigeuner*, *Der Fischerknabe*, *Enfant, si j'étais Roi*, *Es muss ein Wunderbares sein*, *Die Vätergruft*, and many others, Liszt has produced gems, the charm of which is absolutely irresistible to an unprejudiced hearer. He always strives for the closest agreement of the music with the sentiments expressed by the poetry; in this he resembles Franz, and yet how different are the idiosyncrasies of the two masters! This intimate union of two sister arts is due to the same principle which led Wagner to create his stupendous Musical Drama (though he combines with them a third art, that of the theatre), and it forms the link which connects Liszt with his greatest contemporary, however far Liszt's tendencies were removed from the drama.

Although Liszt's principle with regard to both the melodious and rhythmical structure of his songs is that of the most unlimited freedom, yet he often achieves his greatest effects by purely melodious means. Numerous instances of this are pointed out in the footnotes of this volume, to which the reader is referred for further details.

The poems for his songs Liszt selected from the lyrical literature of Germany, France, Italy, and Hungary. Thoroughly polyglot as the sources of his lyrics seem to be, they are so only by the letter, not in spirit, because he was ever striving to reconcile the contrasts in his nature and to refine his conceptions in the fire of his unceasing artistic activity. At the head of the German poets from whose works Liszt chose his texts, we find Goethe and Schiller, and beside these immortals we meet with frequency only Heine and Hoffmann von Fallersleben. From the works of Uhland, Geibel, Herwegh, Rückert, Redwitz, Lenau, and others he has set to music only one poem in each case. Among French poets Victor Hugo attracted him more than any other. The setting of *Angiolin dal biondo crin*, a charming poem by the Marchese Cesare Bocella, was, in the first instance, probably due to his personal relations with the poet.

*Carl Armbruster.*

# BIBLIOGRAPHY

## Biography in English

BEAUFORT, Raphaël Ledos de: Franz Liszt, the Story of his Life. Boston, Oliver Ditson Company, 1910

HABETS, Alfred: Borodine and Liszt. New York, Charles Scribner's Sons

HERVEY, Arthur: Franz Liszt and his Music. New York, John Lane Company, 1911

HUNEKER, James L.: Franz Liszt. New York, Charles Scribner's Sons, 1911

NOHL, Ludwig: Life of Liszt. Translated by G. P. Upton. New York, Charles Scribner's Sons

RAMANN, Lina: Franz Liszt, Artist and Man, 1811–1840. Translated by E. Cowdery. London, 1882

WOHL, Janka: Recollections of Liszt. By a Compatriot. Translated by B. P. Ward. London, 1887

## Biography in German

CHRISTERN, ——: Franz Liszt. Leben und Werke. Hamburg, 1841

GÖLLERICH, August: Franz Liszt. Berlin, Marquardt & Co.

KAPP, Julius: Franz Liszt. Berlin and Leipzig, Schuster & Loeffler, 1909

LA MARA, Marie Lipsius: Liszt und die Frauen. Leipzig, Breitkopf & Härtel

LISZT, Franz: Gesammelte Schriften. 6 Bände. Leipzig, Breitkopf & Härtel

LOUIS, R.: Franz Liszt. Berlin, 1900

POHL, R.: Franz Liszt. Studien und Erinnerungen. Leipzig, 1883

REUSS, Eduard: Franz Liszt. Ein Lebensbild. Dresden, 1898

SCHILLING, G.: Franz Liszt. Eine Biographie. Stuttgart, 1884

VOGEL, B.: Franz Liszt. Leipzig, 1888

## Correspondence

FRANZ LISZT'S Briefe. Gesammelt und herausgegeben von La Mara, 7 vols. Leipzig, Breitkopf & Härtel

LETTERS OF FRANZ LISZT. Edited and collected by La Mara. Translated by Constance Bache. London, 1894

BRIEFE HERVORRAGENDER ZEITGENOSSEN AN LISZT, 3 vols. Leipzig, Breitkopf & Härtel

CORRESPONDENCE OF WAGNER AND LISZT, 2 vols. Translated by F. Hueffer. London, 1888

BRIEFWECHSEL ZWISCHEN FRANZ LISZT UND HANS VON BÜLOW. Leipzig, 1898

FRANZ LISZT'S Briefe an die Fürstin Sayn-Wittgenstein. Leipzig, 1901

FRANZ LISZT'S Briefe an eine Freundin. Leipzig, 1901

## Essays and Sketches

FAY, Amy: In Weimar with Liszt (in *Atlantic Monthly*, 1874)

FINCK, Henry T.: Songs and Song Writers. New York, Charles Scribner's Sons, 1900

HAWEIS, H. R.: Personal Reminiscences of Liszt (in *Belgravia Magazine*, 1881 and 1882)

HUEFFER, Francis: Half a Century of Music in England. London

HUNEKER, James L.: Mezzotints in Modern Music. New York, 1899

LA MARA, Marie Lipsius: Musikalische Studienköpfe. Leipzig, 1877

LANGHANS, W.: Franz Liszt (in *Famous Composers and their Works*). Boston, 1891

NEWMAN, Ernest: A Study of Liszt (in *Century Library of Music*). New York, 1900

SPANUTH, August: Franz Liszt (in *Twenty Piano Transcriptions*). Boston, Oliver Ditson Company, 1903

SPANUTH, August: Franz Liszt's Hungarian Rhapsodies (in *Ten Hungarian Rhapsodies*). Boston, Oliver Ditson Company, 1904

STERN, Daniel (Comtesse d'Agoult): Mes Souvenirs

Thematisches Verzeichniss der Werke, Bearbeitungen und Transcriptionen von Franz Liszt. Leipzig, Breitkopf & Härtel

WAGNER, Richard: Ein Brief über F. Liszt's Symphonische Dichtungen. Leipzig, 1857

WALKER, Bettina: My Musical Experiences

# THE FISHERBOY
## (DER FISCHERKNABE)

(Composed in 1835-36?)

*(Original Key)*

FRIEDRICH von SCHILLER (1759-1805)
*Translated by Charles Fonteyn Manney*

FRANZ LISZT
*Edited by Carl Armbruster*

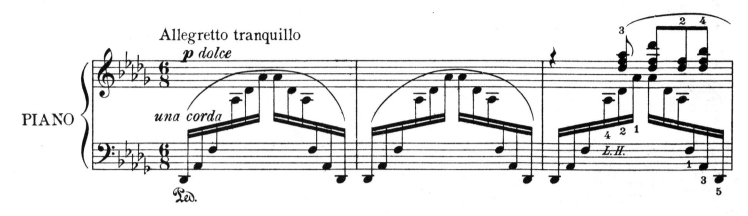

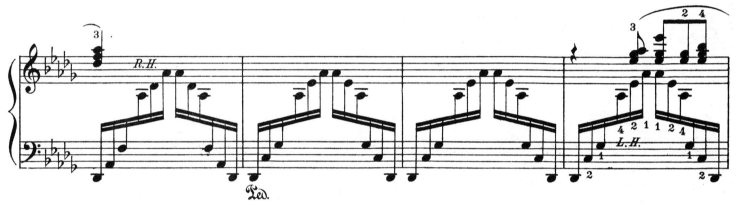

a) It is admissible that part of this measure of rest be filled by the notes sustained by the pedal, but not more than half the measure.

b) Discreetly imitating the singer's expression.

shore ___ Is sleep - - ing and dream - - ing.
ein ___ am grü - - nen Ge - sta - - de.

He hears then a
Da hört er ein

mel - o - dy, Tell - ing of love, As
Klin - gen wie Flö - ten so süss, wie

sweet as the voi - ces of an - gels a - bove.
Stim - men der En - gel im Pa - ra - dies.

a) The music in the left hand here depicts the "dream-melody," so to speak.

4

But when he a - wak - eth From
Und wie er er - wa - chet in

sempre dolce

a)

vis - ions so blest The wa - ters are play - ing O - ver his
se - li - ger Lust, da spü - len die Was - ser ihm um die

cresc.

breast:
Brust.

f agitato

b)

And a voice from the deep calls, "Sweet
Und es ruft aus der Tie - fe: „Lieb'

riten.

un poco più lento
espress.

p

riten.

un poco piu lento

a) Here the dream-melody returns. The right hand accompanying it must ever play softly and impassively, as it were.
b) Mysteriously.

boy,— thou must go, Sweet boy,— thou must go! For mine— is the
*Kna - be, bist mein, lieb' Kna - be, bist mein! Ich lo - cke den*

sleep - er; I lure him be - low, I lure him be - low, I
*Schlä - fer, ich zieh' ihn her - ein, ich zieh' ihn her - ein, ich*

lure him be - low!"— I
*zieh' ihn her - ein."—*

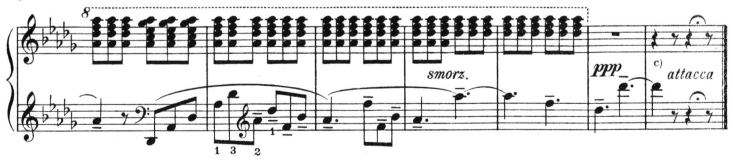

a) Like a harp played at a great distance; a very slight hesitation will add to the effect.

b) Here the original tempo "Allegretto tranquillo" returns. In the left hand the reminiscence of the original should be discreetly prominent.

c) The following song may be enchained if desired.

# THE HERDSMAN
## (DER HIRT)

(Composed in 1835-36?)

*(Original Key)*

FRIEDRICH von SCHILLER (1759-1805)
*Translated by Arthur Westbrook*

FRANZ LISZT
*Edited by Carl Armbruster*

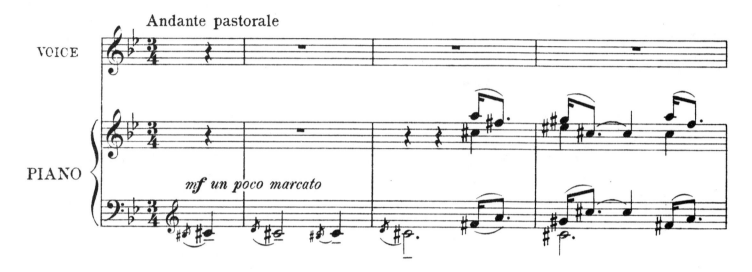

Ye__ mead-ows, fare-well, Fare-well, ye warm sun-ny pas-tures!
*Ihr Mat-ten, lebt__ wohl, Lebt wohl, ihr son-ni-gen Wei-den!*

The__ herds man must__ leave you, The
*Der__ Sen-ne muss__ schei-den, Der*

sum-mer is__ o'er. We go to the
*Som-mer ist__ hin. Wir fah-ren zu*

hills, We come back glad-ly When the cuck-oo calls,
*Berg, Wir kom-men wie-der, Wenr der Kuk-kuk ruft,*

a) The anticipation of the singer's melody with discreet emphasis.
b) Here again the accompaniment anticipates the singer in imitation of the call of the cuckoo.

a) and b)  See notes a) and b) on the preceding page.

c) This passage admits of an increasingly passionate rendering.  The singer grows enthusiastic in anticipating the return of spring.

When the streams___ are flow - ing In bright days of___
Wenn die Brünn - lein flie - ssen im lieb - - li - chen

May.
Mai.

*sempre dolce*

Ye___
Ihr___

mead - ows, fare - well, Fare - well, ye warm sun - ny pas - tures!
Mat - ten, lebt___ wohl, Lebt wohl, ihr son - ni - gen Wei - den!

a) The melody well marked, although "sempre dolce."

The herds - man must leave you, The
*Der Sen - ne muss schei - den, Der*

sum - mer is o'er, The sum - mer is o'er.
*Som - mer ist hin, Der Som - mer ist hin.*

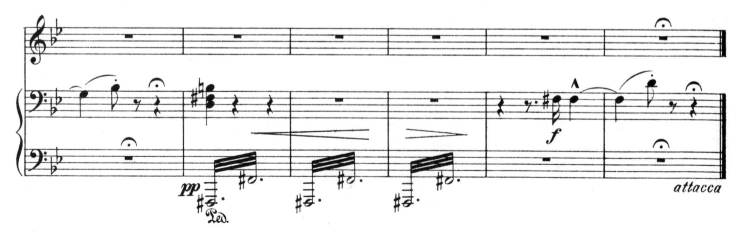

a) The following measures form an introduction to the next song, which should follow without pause.

# THE ALPINE HUNTER
## (DER ALPENJÄGER)

(Composed in 1835-36?)

*(Original Key)*

FRIEDRICH von SCHILLER (1759-1805)
*Translated by Charles Fontcyn Manney*

FRANZ LISZT
*Edited by Carl Armbruster*

a) The sonority of the bass must be governed by the individual power of the singer. The whole song is one of "storm and stress" for the voice; and in order to obtain the necessary contrast, the diminuendos, wherever they occur, may be somewhat exaggerated, i.e. sink down to a real *p* or *pp*.

thun- der the heav'ns, and trem- bles the bridge, The hunts-man is fear-less on
*don- nern die Höh'n, es zit- tert der Steg, nicht grau- et dem Schüt- zen auf*

*sempre f*

*Ped.* *Ped.*

steep, diz – zy ridge. He strides on, un - daunt –
*schwind-li - chem Weg.* *Er schrei - tet ver - we –*

*rinf.*

*Ped.* *Ped.* *Ped.* *Ped.*

– ed, un - daunted o'er gla - ciers and snow, Where
*-gen, ver - we - gen auf Fel - dern von Eis,* *da*

*ff*

smil - eth no sum - mer, where flow'rs nev - er grow.
*pran- get kein Früh - ling, da grü - net kein Reis.*

*marcato* *Ped.*

a) Here lies the climax of the whole composition.

a) The chords not too strongly marked, and this and the next four measures *p* in the accompaniment and *sotto voce* in the voice, so as to give full effect to the closing sentence and afterlude.

# BREATHE GENTLY, MY SONG
## (KLING LEISE, MEIN LIED)

(Composed in 1839)

(Original Key)

NORDMANN
*Translated by Charles Fonteyn Manney*

FRANZ LISZT
*Edited by Carl Armbruster*

a) The exact tempo must be left to the individual taste and feeling of the singer. The pianoforte part is quite subordinate to the voice for the greater part of the song.

way to her win - dow ten - der - ly take,  Breathe
*hut - sam zu ih - ren Fen - stern hin - auf*  *kling*

gen - tly, my  song,_____  nor cause her to a - wake!
*lei - se, mein Lied,_____*  *und we - cke sie nicht auf,*

Breathe gen - tly, my  song,
*kling lei - se mein Lied,*

let each mel - low  tone_____  En - treat my dar -
*kling lei - se und sacht,_____*  *dass die Ge - lieb -*

a) The melody in the bass discreetly prominent, *quasi Violoncello.*

a) The tempo of this portion of the song should be taken so that now a quarter equals a half-note of the previous tempo. The triplets are not to be hurried.

rose___ sings his rap-tu-rous ser - - - e-nade.
*Ro - se ein klin-gen-des Ständ - - chen bringt.*

Ah, wak-en her not___ with too storm-y ca - ress; Like a pil-grim soft-
*Er-we-cke sie nicht___ mit zu stür-mi-schem Gruss, tritt be-hut-sam nur*

shod, draw thou near___ to bless, As en-t'ring de-vout-ly a
*auf wie des Pil - gers Fuss, der hin-durch den hei-li-gen*

tem - ple fair, So sound then my song, like a low mur-mur'd
*Tem - pel geht, still klin-ge dein Gruss wie ein lei - ses Ge-*

a) This anticipation of the new melody, very discreetly. The singer must note the *sotto voce*.

a) From here during the next five measures *accelerando* and *poco crescendo*, both in voice and accompaniment.

a) The *sempre più p* and *perdendo* must be equally distributed over the remaining measures, so that the whole dies away imperceptibly.

# ANGEL FAIR WITH GOLDEN HAIR
## (ANGIOLIN DAL BIONDO CRIN)

(Composed in 1839)

(Original Key, F)

Marchese CESARE BOCELLA
*Translated by Charles Fonteyn Manney*

FRANZ LISZT
*Edited by Carl Armbruster*

a) A song full of naïve charm; it should be rendered simply and unaffectedly, in a tempo not too slow.

*dolce*

flow'r.      May soft breez-es gen-tly
*fior.*      *Che del sol t'in-do-ri un*

*a tempo*
*sempre dolcissimo*

fan    thee, While the sun's bright beams ca - ress   thee; May   the stars shed ra - diance
*rag*    *gio che be-nign' au-ra del cie*    *lo ∨ ti*    *car-rez - zi in sul - lo*

*simile*

*poco rit.*        *a tempo*

rare,   An - gel fair with gold - en hair,      An - gel fair_____ with gold - en
*stel,* ∨ *An-gio-lin dal bion-do crin,*      *An-gio-lin*_____ *dal bion-do*

*poco rit. smorzando*      *a tempo*

∨ *poco rit.*

hair, Love-ly im-age of__ a flow'r.
*crin,* ∨ *bel-la i-ma-gi-ne*__ *d'un fior.*

*poco rit.*      *a tempo*

a)   The melody discreetly (not obtrusively) prominent.

a) The change of melody might tempt the singer to a more dramatic expression: this should be avoided.

b) The accompaniment from here to the end of the song is worthy of study, being not quite so easy as it appears.

a) Note the word *lusingando*

a) In this and the next two measures a *ritenuto a piacere* is permissible, sanctioned by the composer's words "con grazia."

# A WONDROUS RAPTURE MUST IT BE
## (ES MUSS EIN WUNDERBARES SEIN)

(Composed in 1839)

(*Original Key*)

OSKAR von REDWITZ
*Translated by Charles Fonteyn Manney*

FRANZ LISZT
*Edited by Carl Armbruster*

a) One of the most generally admired of Liszt's songs. Its simplicity of utterance demands a corresponding simplicity in rendition, yet expressive of deepest feeling.

a) Note that the arpeggio is prescribed in the bass only. Throughout the song the player must be careful *not* to make arpeggios where they are not marked, and must exercise the utmost discretion in the use of the Pedal.

# THE VIOLET
## (DAS VEILCHEN)
(Composed in 1839)

*(Original Key)*

JOSEPH MÜLLER
*Translated by John Bernhoff*

FRANZ LISZT
*Edited by Carl Armbruster*

a) A song in praise of the Virgin Mary, to whom the month of May is specially dedicated. The poet gives to this and another poem "Schlüsselblümchen", the joint title: "Mutter-Gottes Strässlein zum Maimonate" (A May-Wreath for the Virgin).

b) Sing simply, unaffectedly, with a certain strict adherence to the regular time-beats—not in a *tempo rubato* manner. Liszt intends the "Andantino" to convey not slower, but faster, than "Andante", so that the song may not drag nor be lugubrious.

Nev - er were thy fond de - sire,___
sind nicht dei - ner Schön-heit Zier,___
Yet no sap - phire e'er out
in dem ein - fach blau - en

shone thee, In thy sim - ple blue at - tire.
Klei - de prangst du ed - ler als Sa - phir.

sempre dolce

Neath the hedge-row sweet-ly blow - ing, Know-est not thy vir-tues rare, But thy
Stil - le blühst du und be - schei - den dei - ner Tu - gend und be - wusst, ein - sam

sempre dolce

heav'n-sent breath be - trays thee, With thy head__ bow'd as in-pray'r.
willst du ger - ne woh - nen al - ler Men - schen Freud und Lust.

pp

heart, and lov - ing thee.
*schei - den, keusch und rein.*
Let me like that blue - eyed flow - 'ret,
*Lass mich wie die blau - en Blüm-chen*

With my head low bent___ in pray'r,
*im - mer sanft sein, fromm___ und gut,*
Kneel - ing at Thy feet a - dore Thee, Liv-ing
*dir,___ Ma - ri - a, stets zu Eh - ren le - ben*

ev - er neath Thy___ care, Liv - - ing ev - er neath Thy___
*un - ter dei - ner___ Hut, le - - ben un - ter dei - ner___*

care.
*Hut.*

# THE KING OF THULE
## (DER KÖNIG VON THULE)

(Composed in 1841)

(Original Key, F minor)

JOHANN WOLFGANG von GOETHE (1749–1832)
Translated by Arthur Westbrook

FRANZ LISZT
Edited by Carl Armbruster

There was a King___ in Thu-le, Aye faith-ful to the
Es war ein Kö-nig in Thu-le, gar treu bis an sein

grave,___ To whom his dy-ing la-dy Then a gold-en beak-er
Grab,___ dem ster-bend sei-ne Buh-le ei-nen gold'-nen Be-cher

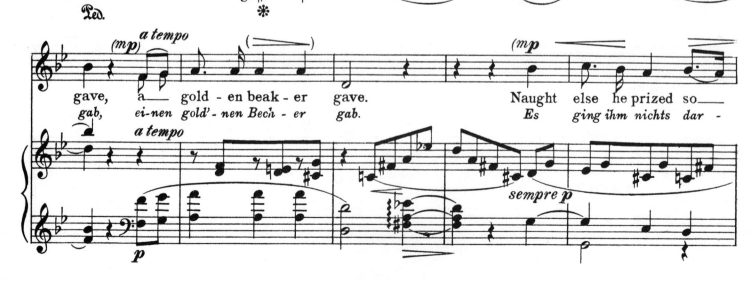

gave, a gold-en beak-er gave. Naught else he prized so___
gab, ei-nen gold'-nen Bech-er gab. Es ging ihm nichts dar-

All on his heirs be - stow - ing
*gönnt' al - les sei - nen Er - ben,*

Ex - cept the cup of
*den Be - cher nicht zu -*

gold,
*gleich,*

All on his heirs be - stow - ing Ex - cept the cup of
*gönnt' al - les sei - nen Er - ben, den Be - cher nicht zu -*

gold.
*gleich.*

He sat at roy - al ban - quet
*Er sass beim Kö - nigs - mah - le,*

A - mid the knightly
*die Rit - ter um ihn*

train,
*her,*

In his an - ces - tral cas - tle
*auf hoh - em Vä - ter - saa - le,*

High tow - 'ring o'er the
*dort auf dem Schloss am*

a) Play this and the next two phrases dreamily.
b) Here the music becomes heroic and majestic, demanding the most sonorous treatment. If the pedal marks are carefully observed there will be no danger of overpowering the singer.

a) With brilliance and dash.
b) Here the fortissimo begins to diminish and the tempo to slacken.
c) To avoid overpowering the singer, $f$ in the right hand and $mf$ in the left.

38

a) This is the musical image of the throwing of the goblet. Play the passage molto crescendo ed accelerando, giving full, or even more then full value to the rest at the end of the next measure; a "speaking" rest.

Then closed his eyes, ne'er to o - - - pen,
*Die Au - gen thä - ten ihm sin - - - ken.*

a)

And nev - er a - gain drank he,
*Trank nie___ ei - nen Trop - fen mehr.*

nev - er a - gain drank he.
*trank nie ei - nen Trop - fen mehr.*

a) The tempo returns to the original Allegretto.
b) This phrase even slower than the preceding one; but the second "never again drank he" must be sung in strict time.

c) The melody is  and not

# O THOU WHO FROM HEAVEN ART
## (DER DU VON DEM HIMMEL BIST)

(Composed in 1841)

(Original Key, E)

JOHANN WOLFGANG von GOETHE (1749–1832)
Translated by Charles Fonteyn Manney

FRANZ LISZT
Edited by Carl Armbruster

Ah,
*Ach!*

of striv-ing I am wear - y,
*ich bin des Trei - bens mü - de,*

Ah,
*Ach!*

of striv - ing I am wear - y,
*ich bin des Trei - bens mü - de,*

What a-
*was*

vails all this wild un - rest?
*soll all der Schmerz und Lust,*

What a-
*was*

a) The melody in the left hand discreetly marked.
b) See a).

vails all this wild un - rest?
soll all der Schmerz und - Lust?

Come, thou long'd
Sü - sser Frie -

for, come sweet peace, and calm
- de, komm, ach, komm in mei -

my breast.
ner Brust.

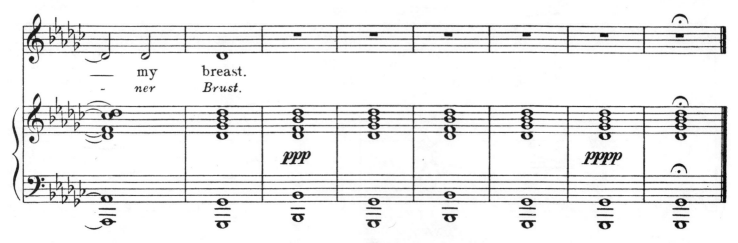

a) The modulation here finely depicts the peace the poet is praying for.

# MIGNON'S SONG
## (MIGNON'S LIED)

(Composed in 1841)

*(Original Key)*

JOHANN WOLFGANG von GOETHE (1749-1832)
*Translated by Charles Fonteyn Manney*

FRANZ LISZT
*Edited by Carl Armbruster*

Molto lento e con ardore

Dost know the land where-in the cit-rons bloom? Like
*Kennst du das Land wo die Ci-tro-nen blüh'n, im*

gold the or-ange gleams thro' leaf-y gloom;
*dun-keln Laub die Gold-o-ran-gen glüh'n,*
A gen-tle wind from
*ein sanf-ter Wind vom*

az-ure heav-en blows, And with the myr-tle high the lau-rel grows.
*blau-en Him-mel weht, die Myr-the still und hoch der Lor-beer steht?*

a) The singer need scarcely be told that this song demands more than to render the notes correctly and observe the marks of expression; it must be imbued with poetry and imagination.

b) The player must carefully distinguish between the chords marked *arpeggiando* and those *not* so marked. The accompaniment is quite as important as the vocal part, but it should naturally never predominate at the expense of the other.

c) The ⌢ merely signifies a breathing space, so to speak.

Dost know it well?
*Kennst du es wohl?*

Dost know it well? Dost know it well?
*Kennst du es wohl? Kennst du es wohl?*

'Tis there, 'tis there, 'tis there_____ I would with
*Da - hin, da - hin, da - hin_____ möcht' ich mit*

*sempre una corda*

thee, my dear-est one,____ re-pair, 'Tis there, 'tis there, 'tis
*dir, o mein Ge - lieb - ter, zieh'n; da - hin, da - hin, da -*

a) Here the piano is to indicate and hold the exact tempo.

a) The ⌢ not coming on the chord, but after it, means that the chord is to have its proper duration and no more, (not forgetting the rallentando). If the singer feels that a prolonged pause on the last two notes in the measure is necessary, the chord must die away before the next measure begins.

b) The arpeggios in strict regularity.

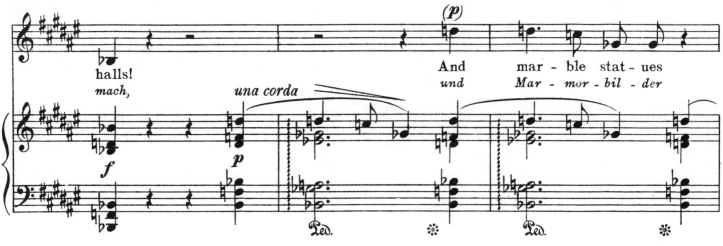

halls!
mach,

And mar - ble stat - ues
und Mar - mor - bil - der

watch-ing si - lent - ly
stehn und sehn dich an:

Would ask "Poor child, is fate un - kind to
was hat man dir, du ar - mes Kind, ge-

thee?"
than?

Dost know it well?
Kennst du es wohl?

Dost know it well?
Kennst du es wohl?

Dost know it well?
Kennst du es wohl?

a) Mark distinctly the original melody, though not obtrusively.  Be careful that the piano part on this page does not drown the low notes of the singer.

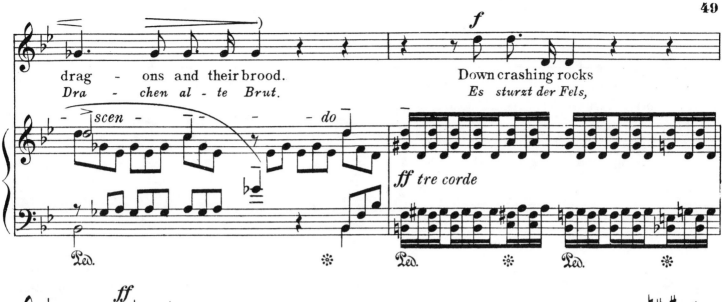

drag - ons and their brood.     Down crashing rocks
*Dra - chen al - te Brut.*     *Es sturzt der Fels,*

rush - es the foam - ing flood.
*und ü - ber ihn die Fluth.*

Dost know it well?      Dost know it well?____
*Kennst du ihn wohl?*      *Kennst du ihn wohl?*____

____ Dost know the land;____ dost know the house,____ the moun - tain
*Kennst du das Land?*____ *Kennst du das Haus?*____ *Kennst du den*

a) These broken chords to be played quite ethereally.

# THE LORELEY
## (DIE LORELEI)
(Composed in 1841)

*(Original Key)*

HEINRICH HEINE (1799-1856)
*Translated by Arthur Westbrook*

FRANZ LISZT
*Edited by Carl Armbruster*

a) This dramatic introduction will be readily understood by those who know from the "legend of bygone ages" that Loreley was an unfortunate maiden who had bravely borne unheard of grief and pain long before revenge and despair had fettered her to the rock from which she looks down upon the broad river.

b) The player must regard these slurs most carefully.

haunts me, nor will it go.
*kommt mir nicht aus dem Sinn.*

The air is cool, day is
*Die Luft ist kühl, und es*

wan - ing, And gen - tly,
*dun - kelt und ru - hig,*

a) From this point to the change into B♭ the accompaniment must be played with great regularity, suggestive of the flowing river. This need not, however, interfere with giving due expression to the melody.

gently flows the Rhine, And gently flows the
*ru - hig fliesst der Rhein, und ru - hig fliesst der*

Rhine, The sum - mits of
*Rhein. der Gip - fel der*

loft - y mountains With
*Ber - ge fun - kelt im*

sun - set splen - dors shine, With
*A - bend - son - nen - schein. im*

a) The tempo of this exquisite Cantilena may perhaps be slightly accelerated.

a) Perhaps this phrase suggests the maiden's song, and may be rendered with some passion.

a) Brilliantly and *strepitoso*. In the following measures pay strict heed to the little diminuendo and crescendo signs.

a) Not a tremolo, but ordinary sixteenths, which against the triplets of the bass produce quite enough disturbance.
b) Not until this point does the disturbance abate.
c) The pause should be long, and then the voice begins simply and sadly.

a) Here the composer permits an optional cut of ten measures.

a) The lower notes are perhaps preferable as being more in keeping with the general tone of the poem.

# IN THE RHINE, THAT NOBLE RIVER
## (IM RHEIN, IM SCHÖNEN STROME)

(Composed in 1841)

*(Original Key)*

HEINRICH HEINE (1799-1856)
*Translated by Arthur Westbrook*

FRANZ LISZT
*Edited by Carl Armbruster*

a) The melodious phrase, rising and falling, may suggest the festive ringing of the cathedral bells, while the incessant roll of sixteenth-notes may represent the waves of the river.

tow - - er,     Co - logne's_____ ma -
Do - - me     Das gro - sse, das

jes - - tic fane.
heil' - ge_____ Cöln.

With -
Im

in,    that might - y tem - ple
Do - me steht ein Bild - niss

Treas - ures a pic - ture so bright,
*Auf gold - nem Le - der ge - malt:*

*più moto*

That o'er my life's sad jour - ney
*In mei - nes Le - bens Wild - niss*

*cresc.*
*tre corde*

*p dolce*

'Tis shed - ding,
*Hat's freund - lich,*

*poco rall.*

*pp*

shed - ding a ray of light.
*freund-lich hin - ein ge - strahlt.*

*colla voce* *dolciss.* *una corda* *pp*
The
*Es*

*sempre pp*

*a tempo*

an - gels hov - er with flow - ers A - round Our La - dy
schwe - ben Blu - men und Eng - lein Um uns - re lie - be

there,
Frau,

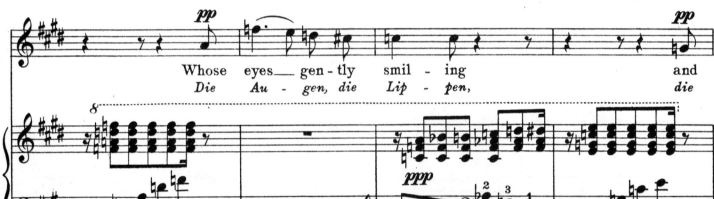

Whose eyes___ gen - tly smil - ing ___ and
Die Au - gen, die Lip - pen,  die

lips___ so sweet Re - sem - ble my dar - ling so
Wän - ge - lein, Die glei - chen der Lieb - sten ge -

# O IN MY DREAMS
## (OH! QUAND JE DORS) [a]

(Composed in 1841-42)

*(Original Key)*

VICTOR HUGO (1802-1885)

FRANZ LISZT
*Edited by Carl Armbruster*

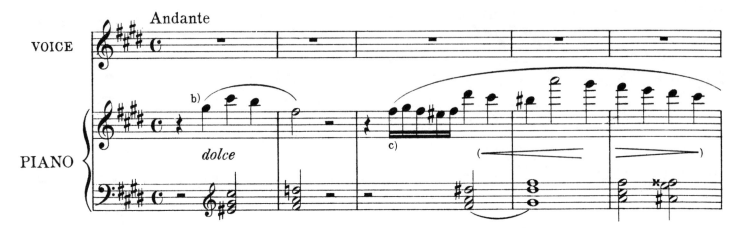

a) In this song Liszt has exactly hit the character of the French Romance with the gracefulness and elegance of his melody and modulations.

b) The player is anticipating the melody, as must be evident in playing and phrasing.

c) The turn deliberately and not too fast.

a) The melody discreetly prominent.

a) and b)  See a) preceding page.

c) The melodic answers in the bass with due importance.   The pedal marks must be strictly observed.

glance from those eyes so ca-ress - - ing, And all my
*gard comme un a - stre s'é - lè - - ve Et sou-dain mon*

*cresc.*

(Andante) *f* *ff*

sor-row will be dis-pell'd,____ And all my
*ré - ve Ray - on - ne - ra,____ Ray - on - ne -*

a) *ff*

*tre corde*

(senza ritardare) (long pause) *pp*

sor-row, all ____ dis-pell'd! Bend to my
*ra!____ Puis, sur ma*

*una corda*

*pp*

b) *staccato*

lips,____ as a vis-ion from heav - en, Be-come a
*lè - vre où vol-tige u - ne flam - me E-clair d'a -*

a) While through the modulations the *poco a poco più di moto* remains always in force, the original Andante returns here.

b) The composer marks this passage "staccato," yet he prescribes the use of the pedal, which destroys the staccato. His meaning probably is that the pedal shall be used only in the earlier portion of each measure and not after the first half.

woman, an-gel that thou
mour que Dieu même é-pu-

art! Place there a
ra, Pose un bai-

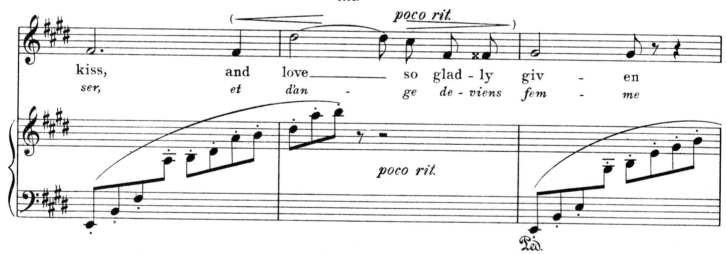

kiss, and love so glad-ly giv-en
ser, et d'an-ge de-viens fem-me

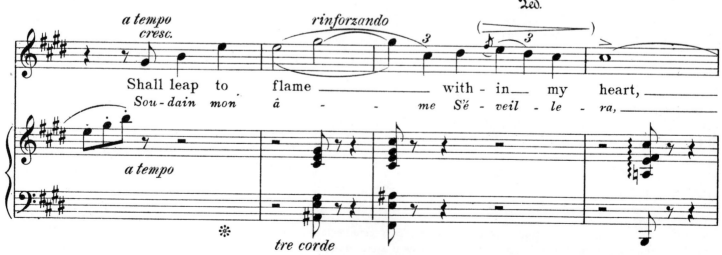

Shall leap to flame with-in my heart,
Sou-dain mon â-me S'é-veil-le-ra,

with - in__ my heart!
S'é - veil - le - ra.

(poco rit.)  una corda  (a tempo)  a)

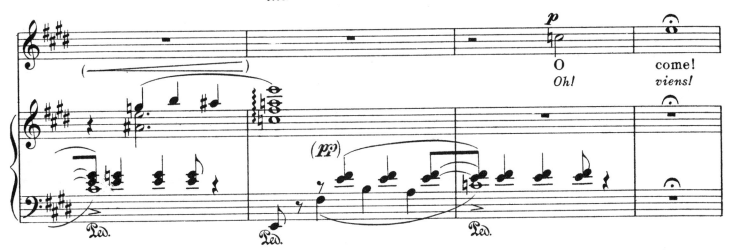

O  come!
Oh!  viens!

*dolcissimo*  *morendo*

as Lau - ra came to Pe - trarch of yore!__
comme à Pé - trar - que ap - pa - rais - sait Lau - ra!__

*pp ritenuto*  *ppp*

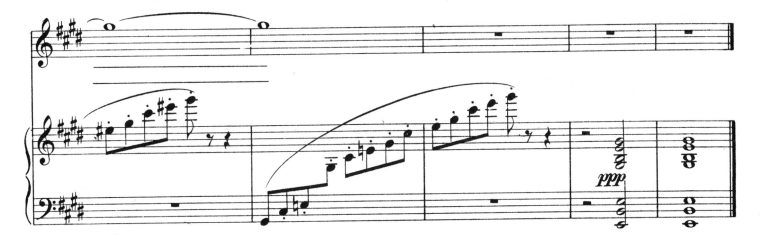

a) The arpeggios rather fast, so as not sensibly to retard the regular flow of the tempo.

# IF I KNEW A MEADOW FAIR
## (S'IL EST UN CHARMANT GAZON)

(Composed in 1841-42)

*(Original Key)*

VICTOR HUGO (1802-1885)
*Translated by Charles Fontcyn Manney*

FRANZ LISZT
*Edited by Carl Armbruster*

a) As long as the running sixteenth-notes continue in the accompaniment the singer should avoid any too marked variations of tempo, so as not to interrupt their regular flow. The whole song must proceed on the lightest of wings.

a) From here to the end of the stanza the singer may be allowed greater liberty in regard to minute gradations of tempo, according to individual feeling.

path I'd make for thee Where thy feet \_\_\_\_ should wan \_\_\_ -
fai - re le che - min Où ton pied \_\_\_\_ se po - - -

*dolce*

der, There a path I'd make for thee Where thy feet\_\_should wan -
se, J'en veux fai - re le che - min Où ton pied\_\_ se po - -

*sf*

- - - der.
- - - se.

*dolce*

*smorz.*

*rit.*

a) Here the original, regular and uniformly flowing tempo returns. The player is cautioned against hurrying this afterlude.

Could there be a dream of love
*S'il est___ un rê - - ve d'a - mour,*

Per - fumed by___ the ros - - es,
*Par - fu - mé___ de ro - - se,*

Where each day,___ with joy in - wove,
*Où l'on trou - - ve cha - - que jour*

Some new charm___ dis - clos - - es;
*Quel - que dou - - ce cho - - - se,*

a) Apart from very slight changes in the voice part, the second stanza is identical with the first; the expression should be the same.

There thy heart should make a nest Where my love___ re-
se, J'en veux fai - - re le nid Où ton coeur___ se

pos - - - es!
po - - - se!

# MY CHILD, WERE I A KING
## (ENFANT, SI J'ÉTAIS ROI)

(Composed in 1841~42)

*(Original Key)*

VICTOR HUGO (1802-1885)

FRANZ LISZT
*Edited by Carl Armbruster*

a) This song calls for rhetorical fire and an exuberance of expression. The hammering eighth-notes of the accompaniment must not impede the singer's tempo-nuances; the latter should, however, not be too sudden.

a) Like a fanfare of trumpets.

a) With the utmost tenderness.
b) The second stanza must form a climax to the first.

a) The thunder in the bass as brilliantly as possible. The trumpet-fanfares, which continue through eight measures, with more and more of festal solemnity.

a) As in a blissful dream.

b) The composer leaves the singer to choose between a half-note (d-flat) or two quarter-notes (c-flat, d-flat). The former way will probably be preferred by the greater number.

# "O HOW," MURMURED HE
## (COMMENT, DISAIENT-ILS)

(Composed in 1841-42)

*(Original Key)*

VICTOR HUGO (1802-1885)

FRANZ LISZT
*Edited by Carl Armbruster*

a) The graceful character of this charming song is essentially French. The nature of the accompaniment suggests the serenade character of the whole.

*) Alguazils—Officers of justice.

a) It will enhance the effect if the suggestion of question and answer is marked. The composer indicates this by marking the questions: "parlando" There should also be a distinction between the answers themselves according to the words: "O row", "O sleep", O love!"

a)   The gradations and nuances of tempo on this page and the following  one must be left entirely to the feeling of the singer.

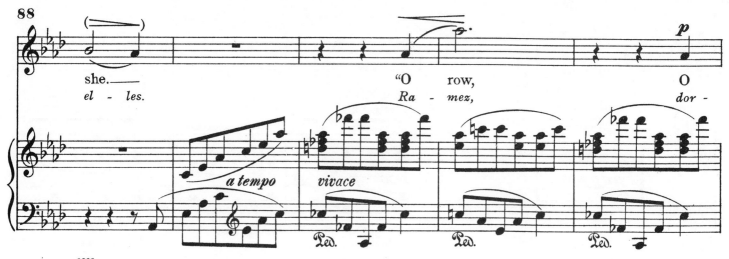

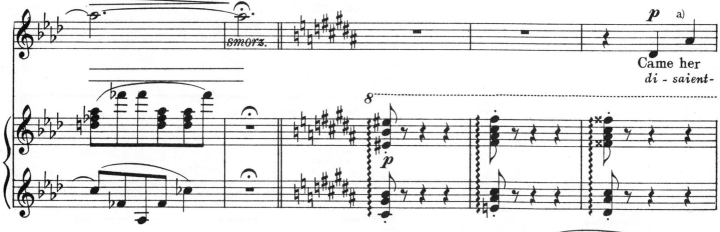

a) Dreamily at first, playfully at the end.

# THE WINDS OF THE AUTUMN
## (ES RAUSCHEN DIE WINDE)

(Composed in 1842)

*(Original Key)*

LUDWIG RELLSTAB (1799–1860)
*Translated by Charles Fontcyn Manney*

FRANZ LISZT
*Edited by Carl Armbruster*

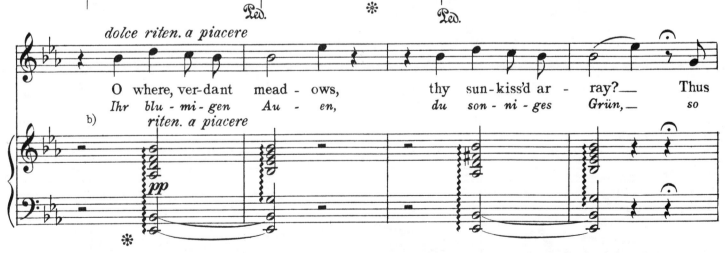

a) Do not take this song too fast. The player must be careful to give the full value to the sustained notes in both hands.

b) Here the mood changes to one of happy recollection; but returns almost at once to the elegiac expression.

life's fair-est blos-soms must with-er a - way, a - way._
wel - ken die Blü - then des Le - bens da - hin, da - hin._

Tempo I

mf
How gray and o'er-
Es zie - hen die

mf pesante

whelm - ing the cloud-mass-es come, And blot out the star - light in
Wol - ken so fin - ster und grau, ver-schwun-den die Ster - ne am

poco rit.

riten. a piacere

heav - en's blue dome.
himm - li-schen Blau.
poco a poco riten. _ _ _ _ _

No more is the
Ach, wie die Ge-
riten.

pp

Ped.　　　　※　Ped.　　　　　　　　　　※

dark-ness dis-pell'd by each ray,___ Thus hope in the bos - om must
stir - ne am Him-mel ent - fliehn,___ so sin - ket die Hoff - nung des

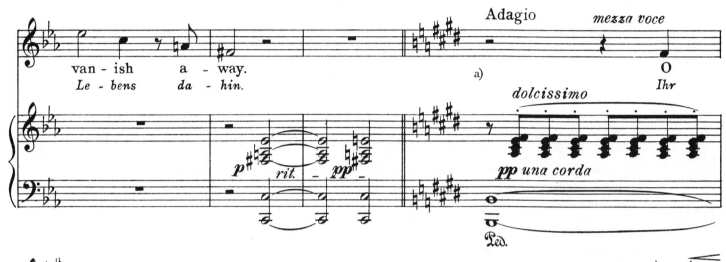

**Adagio**          *mezza voce*

van - ish a - way.          a)          O
Le - bens da - hin.          Ihr

*dolcissimo*

*pp una corda*

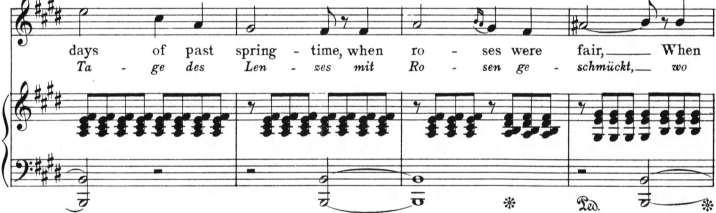

days of past spring - time, when ro - ses were fair,___ When
Ta - ge des Len - zes mit Ro - sen ge - schmückt,___ wo

*un poco stringendo e cresc.* _ _ _ _ _ _

close to my fond heart I held thee, my dear!___
ich die Ge - lieb - te an's Her - ze ge - drückt,___
*un poco stringendo e cresc.*

a) Here the change of mood is more enduring. The contrast of this sunny E major with the gloomy C minor is characteristic of Liszt's method of tone painting, and is as surprising as it is beautiful.

a) *Molto agitato*; i.e. faster than the commencement of the song. The player must raise the pedal at each half measure.
b) These chords most energetically.

a) The expression must be that of overwhelming sadness and the warmest, tenderest feeling.
b) i.e. the tempo of the beginning.

# TAKE OF THE SUN ITS RADIANCE
## (NIMM EINEN STRAHL DER SONNE)

(Composed in 1842)

*Translated by Charles Fonteyn Manney*

(*Original Key*)

FRANZ LISZT
*Edited by Carl Armbruster*

have the self-same fire That burns and sears my in-most soul,___
*hast, was mich er - hellt, und mich er - wärmt und mich ver - klärt___*

*poco rit.*
*rinforz.*

E'er in my be - ing ra - ging
*und was mein in - n'res Le - ben*

*molto appassionato*

*rinforz. e poco rit.*

Till death the flames con - trol!___
*bis in den Tod ver - zehrt!___*

# THE ANCESTRAL TOMB
## (DIE VÄTERGRUFT)

(Composed in 1842)

*(Original Key, F minor)*

LUDWIG UHLAND(1787-1862)
*Translated by Arthur Westbrook*

FRANZ LISZT
*Edited by Carl Armbruster*

a) This song is a true ballad, if we take the word in its real meaning and in the sense of Schubert's and Loewe's ballads. Digni-fied and great in conception, if properly sung the impression it makes is of the deepest. The mysterious phrase at the beginning at once depicts the scene in the most characteristic manner.

b) This is the anticipation of the solemn song of the spirits — it must be played impressively.

a) The song of the spirits.

Un poco più moderato, maestoso

a) *maestoso con portamento*

Ye spir - its of dead
*Wohl hab' ich eu - re*

he - roes, Your greet - ing her - alds my death.
*Grüs - se, ihr Hel - den-gei - ster, ge-hört.*

Of your race the last, I'm
*Eu - re Rei - he soll ich*

a) In spite of the heroic character of the music, the singer must commence *p* and not let himself be carried into the *ff* too soon. This portion – as far as the double bar on the next page – is the climax of the story, and must ring in the hearer's ears long after it has ceased.

a) Here we return to the tempo of the beginning.

ston - y He saw; 'twas yet un-fill'd;      And
Stät - te ein Sarg noch un - ge - füllt,      den

*poco rall.*   *dim.*      *deciso*
*(bestimmt)*

there, as a couch, he laid him,   For pil - low served him his
nahm er zum Ru - he - bet - te, zum Pfüh - le nahm er den

shield.
*Schild.*

Upon his sword he fold-ed His hands, and then fell a-sleep.
*Die Hän-de thät er fal-ten auf's Schwert und schlum-mer-te ein.*

The spir-it voi-ces all van-ish'd,
*Die Geis-ter-lau-te ver-hall-ten.*

And peace reign'd in si-lence deep.
*Da möcht es gar stil-le sein.*

a) The reminiscence of the spirits' song, very softly and slowly.
b) Note the staccato. These closing measures are worthy of Beethoven.

# GAZE UPON ME, EYES OF AZURE
## (SCHWEBE, SCHWEBE, BLAUES AUGE)

(Composed in 1842)

FRANZ von DINGELSTEDT
*Translated by Charles Fonteyn Manney*

(Original Key)

FRANZ LISZT
*Edited by Carl Armbruster*

a) The song dates from the Weimar period, when friendly relations existed between Liszt and the poet, who was then Intendant of the Weimar Theatre.

b) The player must carefully attend to the *arpeggiandos* marked and not be tempted to add others.

a) Reproduce as nearly as possible the *nuances* of the singer.

a) *Quas Violoncello,* and carefully adapted to the vocal part, like the second voice in a duet.
b) See a
c) *Senza Pedale.*

a) Tempo primo, i.e. the tempo of the beginning.

# THOU ART LOVELY AS A FLOWER
## (DU BIST WIE EINE BLUME)

(Composed in 1843)

*(Original Key)*

HEINRICH HEINE (1799-1856)
*Translated by Charles Fonteyn Manney*

FRANZ LISZT
*Edited by Carl Armbruster*

Thou art love-ly as a flow-er, So fair and pure thou art; I look on thee, and sad-ness Steals o'er my yearn-ing heart.

*Du bist wie ei-ne Blu-me, so hold und schön und rein. Ich schau dich an und Weh-muth schleicht mir ins Herz hin-ein.*

*My hands, in ten-der de-*
*Mir ist als ob ich die*

*vo - tion,   I'd rest up-on thy hair,*
*Hän - de auf's Haupt dir le - gen sollt',*

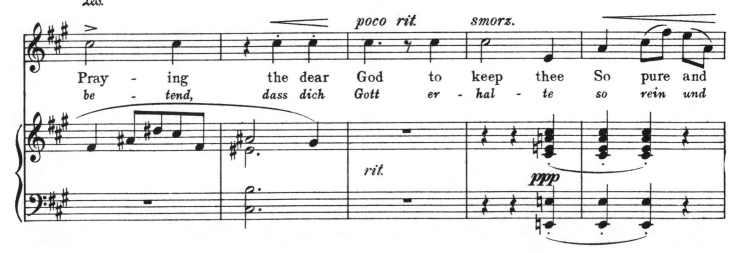

*Pray - ing     the dear God   to   keep   thee   So   pure and*
*be - tend,     dass dich Gott   er - hal - te   so   rein und*

*sweet_____ and   fair.*
*schön_____ und   hold.*

a) Gently marking the reminiscence of the original melody.

# IN NORTHERN LAND A PINE-TREE
## (EIN FICHTENBAUM STEHT EINSAM)

(Composed in 1843)

(*Original Key, C minor*)

HEINRICH HEINE (1799-1856)
*Translated by Arthur Westbrook*

FRANZ LISZT
*Edited by Carl Armbruster*

a) The singer must be most careful of his intonation in these two measures, which are not altogether easy.

A snow - y man - -
mit wei - - sser De - -

poco a poco cresc.

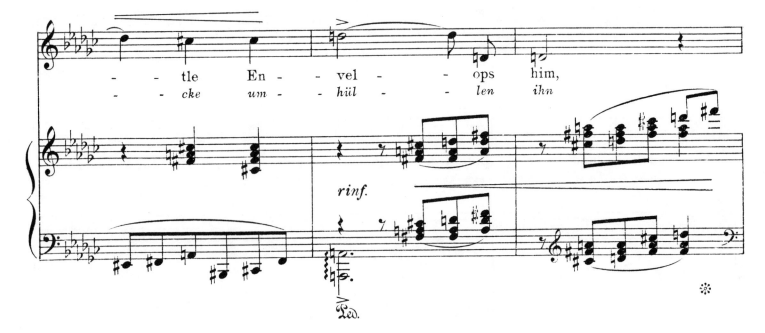

- tle En - vel - - ops him,
- - cke um - - hül - - len ihn

rinf.
Ped.

chill and white.
Eis und Schnee.

rinf.
rinf.
Ped.

marcato
lunga

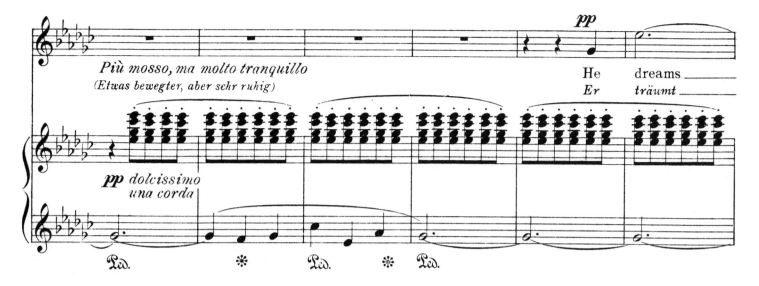

a) The dream melody very tenderly.

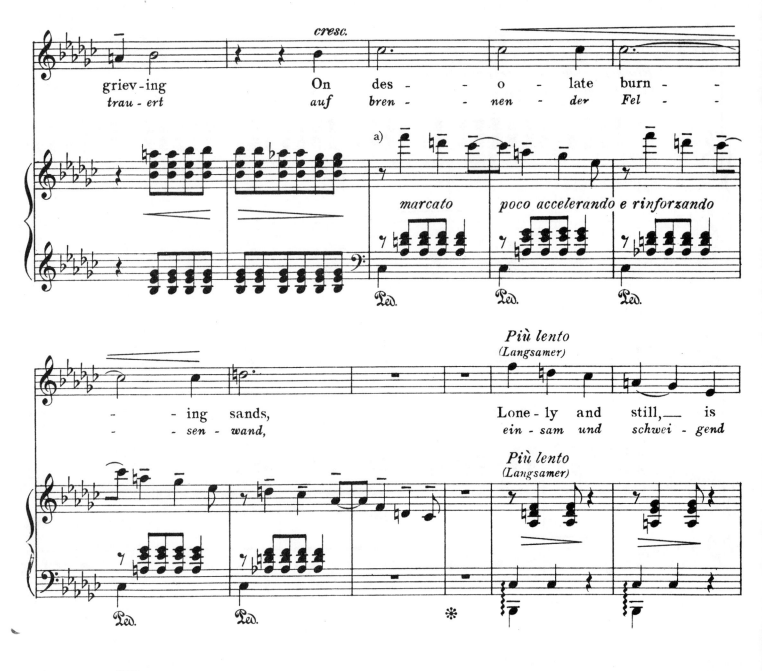

grieving On des-o-late burn-ing sands,
trau-ert auf bren-nen-der Fel-sen-wand,

Lone-ly and still,— is
ein-sam und schwei-gend

griev-ing On des-o-late burn-ing sands.
trau-ert auf bren-nen-der Fel-sen-wand.

a) The accompaniment anticipates the "mourning motive" of the palm-tree, which most fittingly is the same as that of the pine-tree at the beginning.

# JOYFUL AND WOEFUL
## (FREUDVOLL UND LEIDVOLL)

(Composed in 1848)
*(Original Key, E)*

JOHANN WOLFGANG von GOETHE(1749-1832)
*Translated by Charles Fonteyn Manney*

FRANZ LISZT
*Edited by Carl Armbruster*

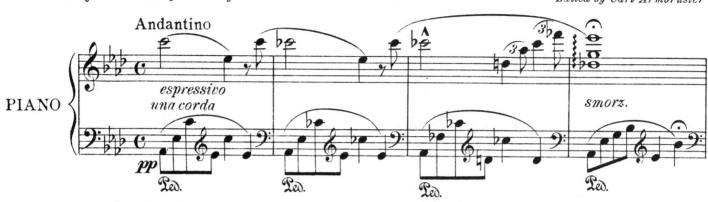

Joy - ful and woe - ful, and thought - ful with care,
*Freud - voll und leid - voll, ge - dan - ken - voll sein,*

Hop - ing, now fear - ing, now swept by de - spair,
*han - gen und ban - gen in schwe - ben - der Pein,*

Caught up to heav - en, then dash'd from a -
*him - mel - hoch jauch - zend, zum To - de be -*

a) The turn slowly and deliberately on the second beat of the measure, making the first note a quarter.

# WANDERER'S NIGHT SONG
## (WANDERERS NACHTLIED)

(Composed in 1848)

(Original Key, E)

JOHANN WOLFGANG von GOETHE (1749-1832)
*Translated by Arthur Westbrook*

FRANZ LISZT
*Edited by Carl Armbruster*

# COULD I ONCE AGAIN CARESS THEE
## (WIEDER MÖCHT' ICH DIR BEGEGNEN)

(Composed in 1850)

PETER CORNELIUS (1824-1874)
*Translated by John Bernhoff*

(*Original Key*)

FRANZ LISZT
*Edited by Carl Armbruster*

a) The beginning of this song, i.e. the two first stanzas must be rendered with a certain diffidence, as if the singer were afraid of uttering the confession of love.   This should, however, not affect the regular flow of the melody, for which the composer even prescribes an accelerando in the fifth measure of the $\frac{3}{4}$ portion.

a) Two sixteenth-notes exactly on the fourth eighth of the measure.
b) See note a).

a) Here the diffidence is at last overcome and the expression changes to that of an open and blissful avowal of love.

b) See note a) on preceding page.

# LET ME LINGER
## (LASST MICH RUHEN)

(Composed in 1855)

(Original Key)

HOFFMANN von FALLERSLEBEN (1798-1874)
*Translated by Charles Fonteyn Manney*

FRANZ LISZT
*Edited by Carl Armbruster*

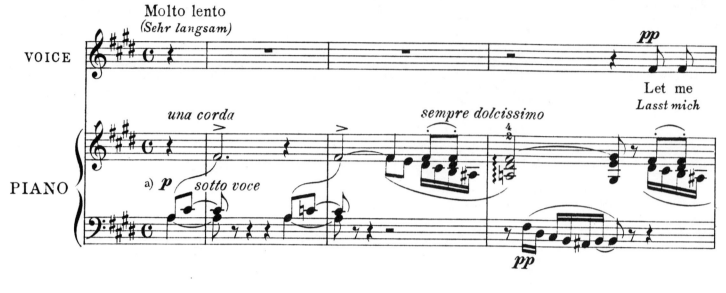

a) In this song, with its warm breath of spring, Liszt has exactly hit the *Stimmung* (mood) of the German poem.   Note the refinement and characteristic nature of the accompaniment as well as the delicate charm of the melody.

la - den,          From the leaf - y shade __ is stream-ing.
*wie - der          in der Zwei - ge Dämm - rung schal - len.*

As the
*Wie des*

a) *sempre una corda*

moon her sil - ver shim — mer To the brook's dark rip - ple
*Mon - des Sil - ber - hel — le auf des Ba - ches dunk - ler*

*poco cresc.*

lend - eth, So this tran - quil hour of e — ven To my
*Wel - le spielt in die - ser lich - ten Stun — de auf des*

a) The triplets not too fast.

lin - - ger, calm - ly dream - - ing, And the
ru - - hen, lasst mich träu - - men bei der

night - in - gale cease nev - - er 'Neath the boughs with blos - soms
Nach - ti - gal - len San - - ge, un - ter vol - len Blü - - then-

teem - - ing, Dream - ing ev - er!
bäu - - men! Lan - ge! lan - ge!

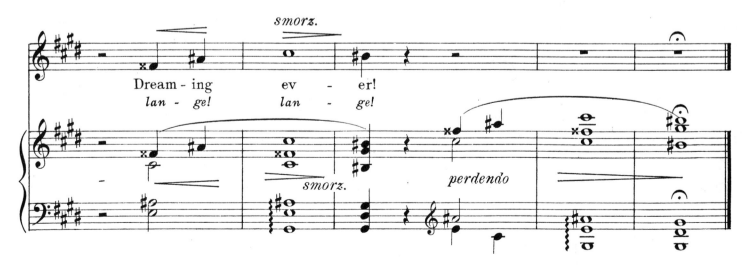

Dream - ing ev - er!
lan - ge! lan - ge!

# IN LOVE'S DELIGHT
## (IN LIEBESLUST)

(Composed in 1857)

*(Original Key)*

HOFFMANN von FALLERSLEBEN (1798-1874)
*Translated by Arthur Westbrook.*

FRANZ LISZT
*Edited by Carl Armbruster*

a) The player anticipates the singer with the melody. It must be done discreetly and without arpeggios.
b) With exuberant passion.

a) The turn very broadly and deliberately.
b) The beginning of the second verse softer than the first one. The tempo is also slightly slower.

a) Senza Pedale, and very softly, though agitato.   The chromatic progressions of the voice must not be blurred by the higher notes in the accompanying chords.

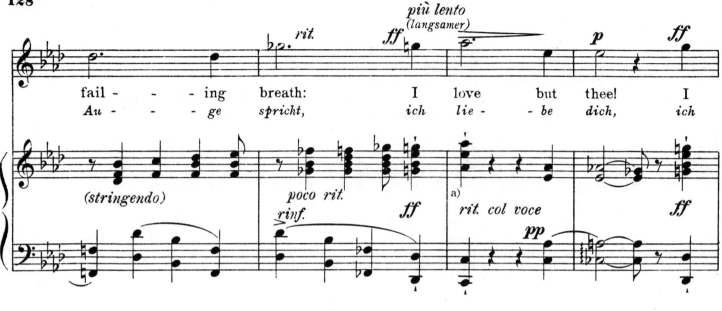

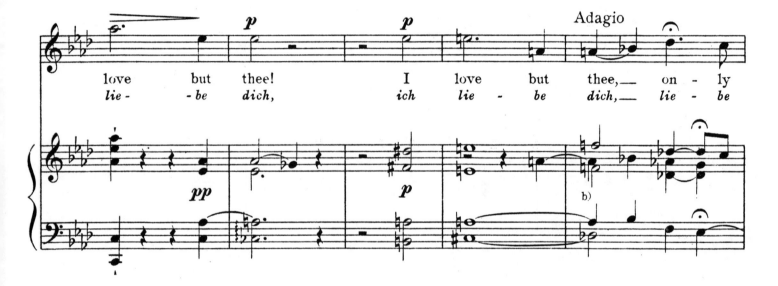

a) The two notes on "I love" (g♮, a♭) always a tempo in spite of the prevailing ritenuto; the latter takes effect after the word "love."

b) Follow the singer implicitly, and make no arpeggios except where indicated.

c) Here we return to Tempo I; the reminiscences of the melody must be played dreamily, and of course very softly.

# I LOVE BUT THEE
## (ICH LIEBE DICH)

(Composed in 1857)

*(Original Key)*

FRIEDRICH RÜCKERT (1788-1866)
*Translated by John Bernhoff*

FRANZ LISZT
*Edited by Carl Armbruster*

a) This song must be very freely declaimed, a task which must be left to the singer's taste. Any metronomic rendition would be altogether unsuitable to its rhapsodic style.

’Tis thus or - dain’d_ a - bove;
nach ei - nem Him - mels - schluss;

I
ich

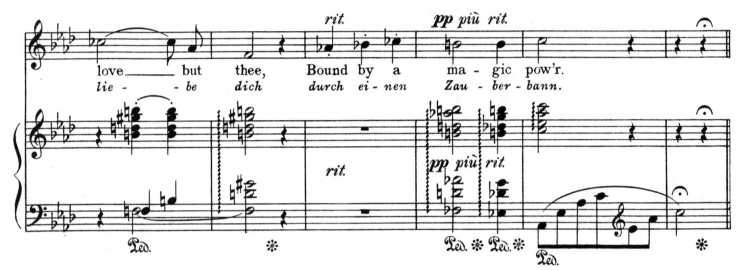

love___ but thee, Bound by a ma - gic pow’r.
lie - - be dich durch ei - nen Zau - ber - bann.

I love thee as the rose___ her leaf - y
Dich lieb’ ich, wie die Ro - - se ih - ren

bow’r,
Strauch,

I love thee, As the sun___
dich lieb’ ich, wie die Son -

a) For concert purposes the Editor strongly recommends the second *(ff)* ending.

# DEPARTURE
## (ICH SCHEIDE)

(Composed in 1860)

*(Original Key)*

HOFFMANN von FALLERSLEBEN (1798–1874)
*Translated by John Bernhoff*

FRANZ LISZT
*Edited by Carl Armbruster*

a) A tender sadness or sweet melancholy (the untranslatable German word *Wehmuth*) is the prevailing mood of this song, as expressed by the composer in his remarkably delicate modulations. A well considered tempo rubato finds a legimate use here.

Fare - well,__ I'm go - - ing."
leb' wohl,__ ich schei - - de.
The
Die

ros - es, just o-p'ning to the light, The lil - ies like an-gels
Ro - sen in ih-rer fri-schen Pracht, die Li - lien in ih-rer

clad in white, The vio - lets sweet-ly blow - ing, Each
En-gelstracht, die Blüm - chen auf der Hai - de, ein

a) This and the next five measures in strict time, or even with a slight accelerando.

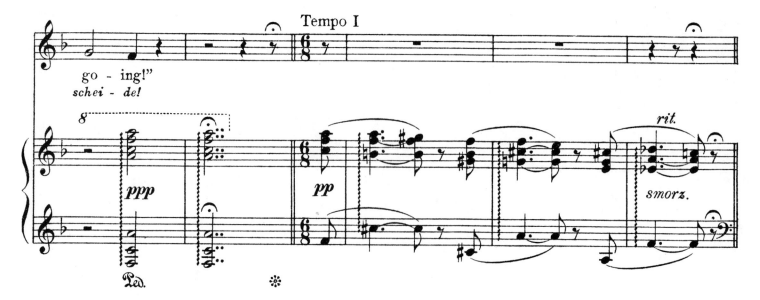

a) Here the tempo rubato returns.

Is life but one e-ter-nal re-frain___ "We part, and shall we meet a-gain?"___ Re-
Ist Al - les nur ein Kom-men und Ge - hen, ein Schei-den mehr, als Wie-der-sehn, ___ wir

joi - cing, weep-ing? No know-ing!          We must be ev - er go -
frew'n uns, hof-fen und lei - den          und müs - sen end-lich schei - -

ing!                     Fare - well,___ we're go - - ing!                     Yes,
den!                     lebt wohl,___ wir schei - - den!                     Und

we must part,     such is our lot,___     Then fare ye well,     for-
muss es denn     ge-schie-den sein___     so le - bet wohl,     ge-

a) This and the next five measures as before.

get me not, Oh, stay___ your tears a - flow - ing, Fare -
den - - ket mein, in Freu - - - den und in Lei - den, lebt

well,___ fare-well, I'm go- ing, Fare-well, I'm go- ing, fare-well, I'm
wohl,___ lebt wohl, ich schei-de, lebt wohl, ich schei-de lebt wohl, ich

ossia

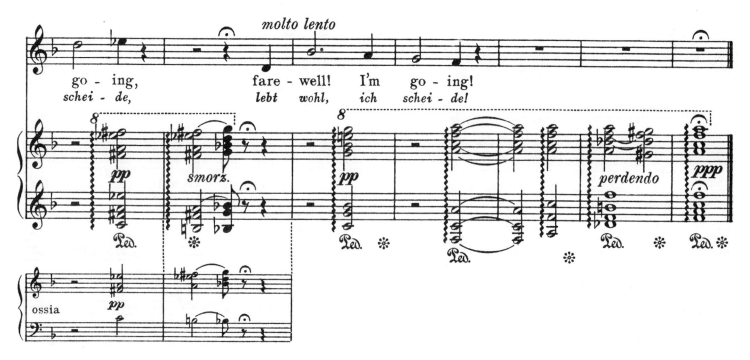

go - ing, fare - well! I'm go - ing!
schei - de, lebt wohl, ich schei - de!

ossia

a) Tempo rubato to the end.

# THE THREE GIPSIES
## (DIE DREI ZIGEUNER)

(Composed in 1860)

*(Original Key)*

NIKOLAUS LENAU (1802-1850)
*Translated by Arthur Westbrook*

FRANZ LISZT
*Edited by Carl Armbruster*

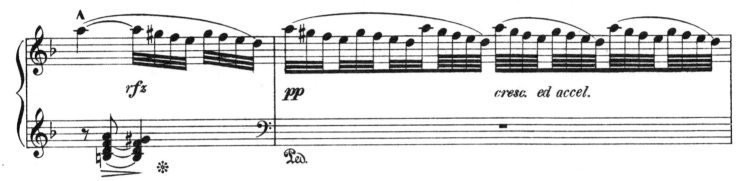

a) It need scarcely be said that the accompanist of this song has quite as important a task before him as the singer. It must be played with extreme brilliancy and dash.

a) It is absolutely necessary that the singer and player thoroughly agree concerning the tempo, as once started, neither can give way to the other without injury to the flow of the whole. Liszt has admirably characterized each one of the three gipsies. Here we have the fiddler and the phrases he plays are strictly Hungarian. They must be rendered with that wild energy peculiar to gipsies, though **pp** all the time.

a) See note a) on previous page.

**Poco lento** (*Etwas langsam*)
*commodo ma deciso* (*phlegmatisch aber bestimmt*)

a) And the sec-ond with pipe__ in mouth,
*Hielt der Zwei-te die Pfeif__ im Mund*

Gaz-ing at smoke__ as-cend-ing,
*blick-te nach sei-nem Rau-che,*

**Più allegro**

Seem'd re-clin-ing in sweet con-tent All__ earth's joys__ tran-scend-ing.
*froh als ob er vom Er-den-rund Nichts zum Glü-cke mehr brau-che!*

a) Here the tempo becomes much slower. We have the portrait of the second gipsy, the smoker, and the accompaniment depicts the smoke as it curls up into the air. The pauses marked must not be too long.

b) It is but natural that the Hungarian National dance, the Czardas, should be introduced, as it lies in the very blood of the whole tribe of gipsies. The tempo quicker than before.

c) With the utmost brilliancy, sonority and "bravura."

d) Here we have the picture of the third gipsy, the sleeper; the tempo again slower.

a) The accompaniment depicts the wind playing upon the strings of the cymbal- in the right hand. The slurred notes in the left, are characteristic cymbal- effects also. Note the *pp, ppp* and *pppp*.

a) The same quick tempo as before. These seven measures will probably be found to be the most difficult for singer and player to keep well together. They should be studied separately.
b) The Czardas tempo as before.

a) Quasi recitativo.

trou - bles to glad-ness. *strepitoso (hastig)*

drei - fach ver - ach - tet.

*dreamily (hinträumend)*

As on I fared I turn'd to look A - gain up-on them

*Nach den Zi - geu - nern lang' noch musst' ich schaun im Wei - ter-*

a) *p un poco pesante*

ly - ing, With hands and fa - ces swart and brown, And their

*fah - ren, nach den Ge - sich - tern dun - kel braun, nach den*

*poco cresc.*

hair slo-ven-ly fly - ing.

*schwarz-lock-ig - en Haa - ren.*

*morendo*

\*) End here, or continue, without the closing chord, to second ending.

a) For the general public the first close will be found more satisfactory than the dreamy, second one, which musicians only will appreciate; at least such was Liszt's personal opinion.